Seasons
of the
Wild

Beaver dam and pond, Canaan Valley National Wildlife Refuge, West Virginia – the 500th Refuge

Seasons
of the
Wild

A Journey Through

Our National
Wildlife Refuges

with

John & Karen

Hollingsworth

Published by:
Worm Press
Post Office Box 235
Bellvue, Colorado 80512-0235

Design: Huffer Design Group, Inc.
Copywriting with: Gina Mohr-Callahan & Gerald Callahan
Seasonal poetry ©1994 Gerald Callahan

Printed in Hong Kong
First edition 1994
ISBN: 0-9636562-5-2
Library of Congress Catalog Card Number: 94-61032

Publisher's Cataloging-in-Publication Data
Hollingsworth, John
     Seasons of the wild : a journey through our national wildlife refuges / with John & Karen Hollingsworth.
     p. cm.

ISBN 0-9636562-5-2
     1. Wildlife refuges-United States. I. Hollingsworth, Karen.
II. Title.
SK361.H65 1994
333.95   94-61032

Acknowledgements

We are most grateful to Bill Kent, Roger Johnson, Rick Coleman, and Mike Smith – all with the U.S. Fish and Wildlife Service – for their advice, encouragement and help during our early days while photographing on the refuges.

We wish to thank the U.S. Fish and Wildlife Service, including the staffs in the regional and Washington offices, as well as refuge managers and their staffs for the advice and assistance they have provided during our years of association.

We greatly appreciate the following members of the Service for their advice, assistance, and encouragement: Nancy Marx, Rob Shallenberger, Nita Fuller, Mike Boylan, Kevin Kilcullen, Don Voros, Nan Rollison, Steve Hillebrand, Tom Nebel, Bruce Blanchard, Dick Smith, Dave Olsen, Megan Durham, and Ken Burton.

We applaud the collaboration we experienced with our designers, Mike and Bonnie Huffer, and the writing and editorial support from Gina Mohr-Callahan and Gerry Callahan. In addition, we thank Gerry for his "season-setting" poetry. We are grateful for the input, encouragement, and efforts of Cathy Thomas, Marie Hedrick, Jan Case, Lynn Udick, Art Rohr, Diane Sanderson, Linda Granberg, and Marvin Cook.

A COMMITMENT TO REFUGES

Photographers John and Karen Hollingsworth and the National Fish and Wildlife Foundation have formed a partnership on behalf of the National Wildlife Refuge System. The Hollingsworths will contribute a portion of the proceeds from the sale of this book to the Foundation to support its conservation work on behalf of the U.S. Fish & Wildlife Service and refuges. These contributions will release an equal amount in matching funds to directly benefit refuges, especially for habitat restoration and environmental education projects.

For more information, write:

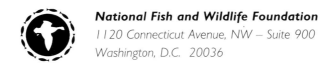

National Fish and Wildlife Foundation
1120 Connecticut Avenue, NW – Suite 900
Washington, D.C. 20036

To Jackson –

*Our friend and companion
who enjoyed most of
these experiences with us.*

We miss you ....

Sunrise on Monopoly Marsh
Mingo National Wildlife Refuge, Missouri

Contents

White ibises at sunset, Merritt Island National Wildlife Refuge, Florida

Introduction

If you're seeking the heart of the wilderness, you'll find it on one of our country's National Wildlife Refuges (NWR). Surely, these are the places that vibrate most intensely with the seasonal movements of wildlife. For the last seven years, we have photographed on more than 400 refuges, and we believe that a season-by-season glimpse into these ever-changing landscapes and ecosystems is the most intimate way to share their amazing variety and wonder.

Let us take you on a journey to some of these rare and precious places. You'll see beribboned spring sunsets streaming out of Arizona's desert heat, carpets of summer wildflowers bright as any dream of Persia, autumn spider webs strung with pearls, and thousands of wintering mallards unraveling their wings like bolts of Chinese silk.

The photographs in this book reflect the beauty and diversity of the habitats and species you'll find throughout the seasons on our nation's

Dragonfly, Santa Ana NWR, Texas

refuges. The accompanying text shares our personal recollections and includes a brief summary about the refuges shown and what you might experience when you visit.

We've seen trumpeter swans bathing in South Dakota's ice-crusted pools. We've watched powerful Kodiak bears feasting on the gifts of an Alaska river. We've come nose-to-nose with alligators bellowing in the heart of the Georgia swamplands. Because of the habitat protection that refuges provide, these creatures still thrive.

A Protected Place for Wildlife

With encroaching civilization diminishing wildernesses, it is critical that we protect natural environments and the splendid mix of species by providing havens where wildlife is the priority, not humans. Refuges are these special places and the least-known of our public lands.

In 1903, President Theodore Roosevelt created

the first refuge, Florida's Pelican Island, to save
herons, egrets, pelicans, and other birds from
millinery plume hunters. Since then, concerned
citizens, private organizations, and government
agencies have worked cooperatively to acquire,
protect, restore, and manage lands for
the conservation of wildlife populations
and their habitats.

There are now more than 500
refuges – an exquisite and ever-
expanding network of more than 91
million acres of diverse land and water
habitat in all 50 states and 8 territories.
The System stretches from Alaska's Arctic
tundra to the Caribbean's azure seas,
from rocky atolls in the South Pacific to
the north woods of Maine. The National Wildlife
Refuge System is unparalleled anywhere for its
size, diversity, and skillful management.

The U.S. Fish and Wildlife Service (USFWS)
manages these refuges, which provide essential
food, water, and living space within countless
ecosystems: more than 60 endangered species and
hundreds of species of mammals, birds, reptiles,
insects, amphibians, fish, and infinite numbers of

Moonrise, Chincoteague NWR, Virginia

plants. Depending on the needs of wildlife, the
USFWS manages each refuge accordingly.

A number of refuges, like Alaska's Kodiak NWR,
are utterly wild and essentially self-managed.
Several refuges would not exist without the precise
intervention of refuge managers and
wildlife biologists. Many refuges are
delicate oases – painstakingly protected
pockets of wildness nestled in the niches
of cities.

Some refuges, like Maryland's
Blackwater NWR, serve as super
highway "rest stops" for migratory birds
on their way to and from nesting and
wintering grounds. Some refuges, like
California's Tijuana Slough NWR, were
established to protect a dwindling species like the
endangered light-footed clapper rail.

Others, like Oklahoma's Wichita Mountains
Wildlife Refuge – established for the American
bison – preserve a precious piece of our country's
history or make environmental education a top
priority like Pennsylvania's John Heinz NWR at
Tinicum.

Still other refuges, like Michigan's Seney NWR, are stellar examples of reclamation – areas that were abused and nearly stripped of their natural resources, then carefully managed and restored to richly diverse wildlife habitat.

Exploring the Refuges

With refuges in all 50 states, chances are, there's a National Wildlife Refuge near you. Besides offering peace and solitude from today's hectic pace, many refuges provide educational, recreational, and volunteer opportunities as well as visitor centers for you and your family.

Grab your binoculars and spend an afternoon birding. Enjoy a workshop in mother nature's classroom, try your hand at wildlife photography, or plan a vacation around a refuge event. There are hundreds of festivals and special activities to choose from – all tracing the seasonal cycles of wildlife. Because events vary with each refuge and the seasons, check **Our National Wildlife Refuges** calendar for detailed monthly listings of refuge activities around the country.

Pronghorn, National Bison Range, Montana

As you explore the refuges in your own state, you'll discover that each refuge has a character all its own. Some are breathtaking and grand, others beckon you to examine their wonders more closely.

Each visit will provide a variety of sights, sounds, and smells. To increase your chances of seeing wildlife in their natural habitats, plan to arrive at dawn or dusk – the prime viewing times. And know that because nature is always unpredictable, each visit will be different from the last, each memory will be different from that of the person in front of you or behind you, each encounter will be different from the next . . . and the next . . . and the next . . . .

Let us be your guide to things wild. Then take a journey of your own to our National Wildlife Refuges.

Be patient. . . be observant. . . be considerate. . . of these rare places.

Spring

. . . something inside of me

*remembers or anticipates
sunflowers, imagines them*

*even now, beneath the earth, coiled
in their black sweaters, waiting*

for the warm fingers of spring.

*A*gain, the planet turns on its great hinge, and the shell of winter splits. Flowers blossom, dragonflies flick on their green and purple motors, and birds grow restless as bees. The trees are rekindled. Just look at the marmots on their rocks or children or frogs. Even the stones are hopeful. It is a time to leave behind the doubts of winter and the easiest time of all to see beyond the ordinary slight of hand, to the true magic, even in the simplest things — sandpipers, dandelions, grass as green as envy, pebbles, clouds, raindrops.

*O**f the birds that spend their lives at sea, the albatross is for me the most evocative of ships and sailors and the azure arc of the sea. Albatrosses and red-footed boobies only come ashore for courtship and nesting and have little fear of people. I move among them like a child – awed by their size and beauty, giggling at their rituals. And around us all, the jet-black precipices of Kilauea and a sea like a fierce green crystal.*

K.H.

Laysan albatross with chick

Kilauea Point National Wildlife Refuge *is perched on the lip of an extinct volcano on the coast of the Hawaiian island of Kauai. Frequent rains have coaxed the green out of these cliffs and mountains and made an ideal spot for seabirds to nest, after literally years at sea. In spring, the refuge is humming with boobies, Laysan albatrosses, wedge-tailed shearwaters, and other seabirds.*

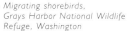 Migrating shorebirds, Grays Harbor National Wildlife Refuge, Washington

Red-footed boobies

$\mathcal{H}$ere, mountains rise from the desert like stone fists. There is little water, less shelter. But at dusk, the light moves like snakes among these peaks, and you can see clearly each of the pigments native peoples used in their pots and their blankets. And in this stark desert, there is life – lizard and kangeroo rat tracks in the morning sand, wildflowers after blessed spring rains, and if you know where to look, desert bighorn sheep – handsome as sandstone and as determined.

K.&J.H.

Desert bighorn sheep

Established in 1939 to protect the dwindling desert bighorn sheep population, **Kofa National Wildlife Refuge** is nearly 1,000 square miles of peaks, canyons, and hills in the harsh Sonoran Desert north of Yuma, Arizona. Spring is a lively and hospitable time to visit. Giant saguaro cacti, chollas, and mesquite dot the area's jagged horizon. Look carefully for desert birds: elf owls, phainopeplas, brown towhees, and cactus wrens.

Saguaro cactus at sunset

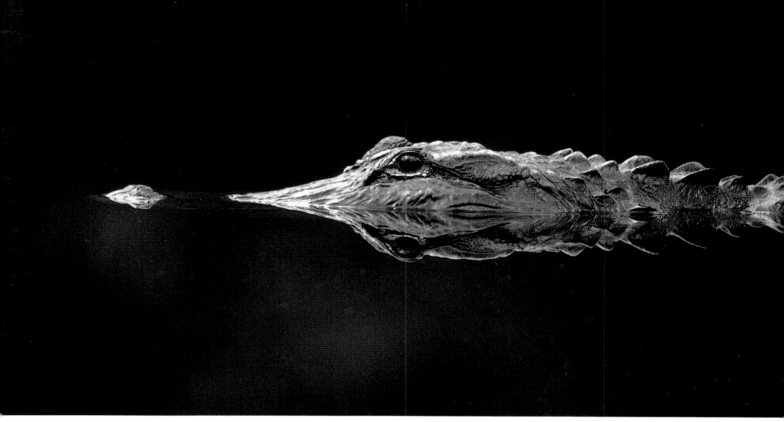

American alligator

ators! Bellowing like an unmuffled two-cycle outboard and no more than 15 feet from our canoe! There must be a nest nearby. Most people avoid swamps, but places thick with water are places thick with life. In spring, there are frogs, snakes, water lilies, and birds that hang in trees like poppies – with songs like flames. But the alligators are the loudest and oldest and oddest of all the creatures here. These reptiles touch us someplace deep and dark.

J.&K.H.

Okefenokee National Wildlife Refuge in southeastern Georgia is a vast, prehistoric swamp. Its nearly 400,000 acres (most of which are wilderness) of freshwater lakes, dotted with islands and shallow prairies are home to an amazing diversity of wildlife and habitat: more than 225 bird species, 42 mammal species, 58 reptile species, amphibians, and fish. You can visit by boat or canoe, and some hiking trails are available, along with swamp boardwalks with observation towers.

Blue-winged teal pair

They crane their necks in this soup like crops of rusty periscopes – as far as you can see. And these cattails quake with the life in the marsh: blue-winged teals like these; muskrats etching new pathways; crickets, fat and black; marbled snakes; belching frogs. There is no place like springtime in a marsh. I like to just sit back and let it tell me all its stories.

K.H.

· · · · · · · · · · · · · · · · · · · ·

Horicon National Wildlife Refuge *is part of one of this country's largest freshwater cattail marshes — formed by a great glacier during the last ice age. Nearly 12,000 years ago, nomadic hunters flocked here because of the area's abundant wildlife — still plentiful today. This Wisconsin refuge is famous for its massive marsh, migrating Canada geese, songbirds, and shorebirds. Between April and September, a refuge access road provides unique opportunities to experience the interior of the marsh itself.*

Horned lizard

The desert floor at dawn seems to move in fits and spurts. Clay-baked bars of earth scuttle and bump, raising puffs of dust as from a magician's hand. Lizards! The desert floor is alive with them! Sunning themselves on the faces of stones, stretching their long tongues in search of food. Exploring with their young and disappearing into the folds of the desert's sheltering cape.

J.H

. . . .

Blunt-nosed leopard lizard

Pixley National Wildlife Refuge is a 6,000-acre, San Joaquin Valley, California upland refuge. It was formed to protect the endangered blunt-nosed leopard lizard, the San Joaquin kit fox, and the Tipton kangaroo rat. A portion of the refuge also serves in the recovery of the area's waterfowl population. If and when water is plentiful, the refuge is literally a desert oasis for wildlife.

White pelicans

I didn't choose these pelicans. From somewhere beyond the dawn's mist, they chose me. I like it that way, always a surprise, always intimate. So many birds feed and fatten here on their way north, there's no way to predict who will come and sit for me or what plumage they will choose. So I bring a lot of lenses and very few expectations. K.H.

Tule Lake National Wildlife Refuge is one of six extremely diverse refuges in the Klamath Basin NWR Complex spanning the California-Oregon border. The area is abundant with constantly changing wildlife all year long. At Tule Lake in spring, the skies are a flurry with waterfowl and shorebirds on their way to Arctic breeding grounds. Thousands of marsh birds and waterfowl nest in the wetlands of Tule Lake, and hawks, owls, and falcons raise their young on the cliffs of Sheepy Ridge.

Standing here in spring, there is an acute sense of the great spiral of life. Overhead, flocks of birds, like clouds, spin frantically north to breed and nest. And all around, among the Kansas marshes, bitterns feed upon frogs and snakes, and in the uplands, finely plumed pheasants dance fierce dances. Here, for me, the cycle turns tangibly, and upon the cusp of each moment, another life is ended or begun.

K.H.

Ring-necked pheasant

Quivira National Wildlife Refuge in south-central Kansas is a major stop for migrating birds in both spring and fall. Shorebirds, white pelicans, sandhill cranes, and an occasional endangered whooping crane often stop here on their treks north and south. Ancient basins — Big Salt Marsh and Little Salt Marsh — lie in the critical "transition zone" of the Flyway, and a wide variety of wildlife dwells here all year.

American bittern with a yellow-bellied racer

Black-crowned night heron

*U*tah's west desert is as forbidding as any. But I can still see where the Pony Express and Overland Stage passed through in the 1800s. Flat and barren as the moon, the desert rolls south to where an immense spring feeds a prehistoric marsh, and birds gather in like spooled wool. The miracle of water is striking as I stand in warm desert sand, watching a black-crowned night heron fishing the afternoon away.

J.H.

Fish Springs National Wildlife Refuge is an extremely isolated area on the southern edge of the Great Salt Lake Desert. This place is steeped in history. The transcontinental telegraph was strung through here, and a refuge cave holds human artifacts dating back more than 11,000 years. A 10,000-acre marsh is a welcome stop for ducks, herons, geese, and other migratory birds. Late spring is an excellent time to visit this desert oasis.

Bison herd

*T*he sheer tonnage of them is awesome enough. 400 nappy bulks, 400 massive heads noshing prairie grasses on the edge of a cliff. And the cowboys yawing and whooping and jostling them forward – over the edge – to their summer range south of the Niobrara River. Once the beasts are in motion, it becomes surreal. Buffalo pouring from the cliff on both sides of me. Great thunderheads of grit. And a sound like the end of the world.

J.H.

Bison, National Bison Range, Montana

Fort Niobrara National Wildlife Refuge is 19,000 acres of rolling prairie grasslands along the Niobrara River in north-central Nebraska. In the 1880s, Fort Niobrara kept the peace between area settlers and the Sioux Indians on the nearby Rosebud Reservation. Today, the refuge's sandhills and breaks are managed for American bison, elk, and Texas longhorn cattle. But the area is also an ideal habitat for whitetail deer, songbirds, burrowing owls, and prairie dogs. Prairie chickens do their exotic dance here in spring, and prairie wildflowers are abundant in early summer.

Green-backed heron

In the sawgrass marshes of southeast Florida, the last of the rivers of grass still flow. A unique ecosystem, the swamp teems with life – plant and animal: spiked bromeliads, ferns, woody vines, anhingas studded with turquoise, purple gallinules. I stand among them almost unnoticed, witness to their daily lives, imbibing all of the smells and sounds that bubble from the mud, and the trees, and the dark warm water.

K.H.

About 221 square miles of northern Everglades, **Loxahatchee National Wildlife Refuge**, near Boynton Beach, Florida, is an abundant bird-life haven. In spring, from the marsh nature trails and cypress swamp boardwalk, you can see spectacular wading birds – egrets, herons, ibises – performing their courtship rituals in their breeding plumage. Alligators are also easy to spot. Late fall through spring are the best times to visit, and photo opportunities are plentiful.

Black-shouldered kite family

There is a space around animals, especially families, that is nearly visible. The animals create this fragile sphere, and I never risk spoiling it. This time, an already established blind allows me a precious chance to climb inside this space and create no fear. The moments with these black-shouldered kites are remarkable. The efforts of the parents, the appetites of the young, and the sacred repetition of it all.

K.H.

On the lower Gulf Coast of Texas, **Laguna Atascosa National Wildlife Refuge** is a unique ribbon of both semiarid and subtropical climes. This creates a tremendously diverse area for habitat and species. You can see everything from prickly pears and mangroves, armadillos and ocelots, to warblers and snow geese. Any time of year is special here.

Summer

Now the Northern door is latched and the cracks between the moments are caulked with essences of mint and wild rose and goldfinch.

Between June and September, we are all naturalists — gathering pebbles, pressing flowers, following fireflies, memorizing the names of birds and trees, marking the paths of spiders among the peonies. And while frogs croak like kettle drums and thunderstorms billow suddenly black, the mountains empty of snow and ice, and buttercups and lupine and columbine blossom like fire. And at night, we become astronomers and measure exactly the light years to Alpha Centauri or the orbits of Io. We verify the past. We imagine the future.

It was a mistake to come here alone. One man on a remote inlet of this Alaskan refuge and 25 magnificent Kodiak brown bears feeding on the river's gifts and sparring on the hillsides. Through the tall and fragile grass curtain between us, I watch them, listen to their snorts, observe their hierarchies, and tremble in awe of their power. Five extraordinary days with only the cries of eagles and the eyes of bears – all around me.

J.H.

Bald eagle

Kodiak National Wildlife Refuge *is a rugged and mountainous island spanning almost 1.7 million acres in southwest Alaska. During the summer and early fall, mighty Kodiak brown bears as well as bald eagles migrate here to feast on the spawning salmon in the area's coastal rivers and streams. More than 200 bird species have been identified here, and they share the refuge with foxes, mountain goats, and other creatures.*

Field of clover,
Rice Lake National
Wildlife Refuge, Minnesota

Kodiak brown bear

Monarch butterflies
on milkweed

It's as if Diego Rivera stopped here to paint a mural on the afternoon air. Sheaths of emerald, grand swaths of molten oranges, rivulets of black, calla lily whites. The monarchs are knee-deep in the milkweed's nectar and oblivious to me and the others around them. The ibises, the stately waders, the cottontails and foxes, the black-crowned night herons sulk in the shadows along my wildlife drive.

J.H.

Eastern cottontail

The Brigantine Unit of the **Edwin B. Forsythe National Wildlife Refuge**, just north of Atlantic City, New Jersey, is a tidal wetlands sanctuary. Each year, tens of thousands of migratory birds make the trip: geese, ducks, wading birds, songbirds, shorebirds, and more. Some stay to nest and raise their young on the refuge's 39,000 acres of shallow bays and salt marshes.

Tarantula hawk on milkweed

*A*rizona in August? You've got
to be kidding! But what I see is absolutely
verdant, the kind of green that hurts your
eyes. The mid-summer monsoons – gathering
up their billowing skirts out of nowhere each
afternoon – have transformed this vast and
wild place into a dream of Wales. The long
dry fuse of this valley has been ignited with
life. A tarantula hawk nectars lazily on
milkweed. There is so much to explore here.
My eyes cannot see it all.

                                          K.H.

Chihuahuan pronghorn

Buenos Aires National Wildlife Refuge
reaches across nearly 114,000 acres of south-
central Arizona, near the Mexican border.
Established in 1985 to preserve habitat for the
endangered masked bobwhite quail, the refuge is
part of the Sonoran Savannah Grasslands. More
than 150 lakes and ponds and Arivaca Creek
attract diverse species – especially subtropical
birds. Chihuahuan pronghorn antelope have been
successfully introduced, and although elusive, the
masked bobwhite quail is gaining a foothold here.

Royal tern colony

hide my camera in my raincoat today, but it isn't raining. In summer, the pitted shores of this refuge are so lush with nests, and chicks, and eggs that we must walk in the ocean's spray to avoid their world. A research biologist steps lightly with me, surveying the nesting colonies of squawking gulls and terns. This stretch of beach is speckled with feathery mounds. J.H.

. . . .

Protected by a barrier island, **Cedar Island National Wildlife Refuge** on North Carolina's central coast is a large salt marsh. It's a hospitable place for wintering ducks and a lively nesting place for brown pelicans, gulls, and terns in spring and summer. Songbirds are abundant during spring and fall migrations.

June days in northern Minnesota are nearly Arctic in length. And the fields here fill up with goldfinches and dragonflies and clay-colored sparrows. So much to see: newly born black bears, wolves, moose, otters, deer, ducks. It was difficult, but I chose one of the three fox dens. It took five days before these pups were comfortable with me.

J.H.

Northern pitcher plant

Agassiz National Wildlife Refuge *is a wild and unique woodland and wetland area of northwestern Minnesota. Once covered by a massive glacial lake, the refuge today includes fluctuating pools, open grasslands, boreal forest, aspen groves, even a quaking bog. The area is rich with wildlife and the only refuge in the lower 48 states with a resident pack of gray wolves. June is a wonderful time to see the extraordinary diversity.*

Red fox pups

Field of lupine

*W*oven on the threads of this valley is a ribbon of wildflowers as brilliant as Van Gogh's fields at Arles. Riots of blue lupine in the meadows, flashes of bluebirds in the air. Trumpeter swans and moose calves sheltered in the crook of the Centennial Mountains' rugged arms. My two weeks of summer in southwestern Montana have been a photographic explosion – trying to paint the shades, the creatures, the sunsets with my camera.

K.H.

Trumpeter swan family

In an extremely remote area of Montana's Centennial Valley lies **Red Rock Lakes National Wildlife Refuge**. The 44,000-acre refuge was established to protect the rare trumpeter swan from extinction. Because of this refuge's success, wildlife biologists are reintroducing these magnificent birds into much of their former habitats. Although difficult to reach, this refuge is worth the trip, especially in summer, when the flowers and birds are profuse.

Le Conte's sparrow

From where I sit in the native grasses and wildflowers of these prairie pothole hills, there is a symphony of wonderful noise. You can't see them, but you can hear them, deep among the woody stems and green-brown stalks. The voices of grassland sparrows and water birds singing their nesting serenades. This is a wild and primal place. If you listen, you can almost hear the echoes of spruce spikes and tamarack wisps percolating under the ice of the Wisconsin glacier – 10,000 years before.

K.H.

. . . .

Upland sandpiper

Lostwood National Wildlife Refuge *is a terminal glacial moraine in the northwest corner of North Dakota, known as Coteau du Missouri – hills of the Missouri. The refuge is a birder's paradise; with nearly 27,000 acres of prairie grasslands punctuated with thousands of pristine lakes and potholes. Le Conte's and Baird's sparrows, upland sandpipers, marbled godwits, and willets are among the many birds readily seen here in early summer.*

hese rocks, strewn like seeds across a remote corner of the Bering Sea, house the nests and rookeries of an unimaginable variety of birds. Birds with magical names like crested auklets, horned puffins, black-legged kittiwakes, and thick-billed murres. The sun never shone during the nine days I was here. But each day was lit by wings of birds and a carpet of wildflowers, bright as any dream of Persia.

J.H.

. . . .

Arctic fox

When the fog lifts off the Aleutian Islands, and you can see a thousand more islands before you, the vastness of the **Alaska Maritime National Wildlife Refuge** is almost incomprehensible. The refuge includes 3.5 million acres, and more than half of these are wilderness. Each year, 40 million seabirds and other bird species come here to nest. Sea and land mammals are plentiful: fur seals, walrus, sea otters, caribou, reindeer, Arctic foxes, brown bears, and wolves. Refuge access can be a challenge, but it's worth it.

Crested auklets

Autumn

Now, I want to live through
just one more autumn.
I want to listen while the wind
uses leaves to speak its
unsayable words.
I want to watch as the sky
fills with corn husks and
wedges of wild geese.

The elk are restless again,
watching the low line of clouds
moving north across the empty
fields, watching the quarter moon
thicken in the darkness above
the rattling cornstalks. In the
trees, in the meadows, the earth
is making plans inside of them,
and the birds are being pulled
further and further south. The air
smells of nutmeg, and leaf-fires,
and the green ice near the poles.
It will snow soon, that miraculous
first snow. Wood will need to be
split and stacked. There will be
bread and the racket of geese
moving south.

Maxfield Parrish blue or maybe sapphire. The fall morning skies here are a remarkable color. Cool – like porcelain dippers full of sweet water. The old sun is in just the right place, but the reflections on this beaver pond last only an instant, brilliant threads flying through shuttles of the loom. Like comets they burn brightly at first, auburn, amber, wine, crimson. Then they smolder, muted trails. Every moment has meaning, and I am afraid to blink.

J.H.

Beaver habitat

Continuing the tradition begun nearly 2,000 years ago, the Chippewa Indians still harvest wild rice from east-central Minnesota's **Rice Lake**, now a **National Wildlife Refuge**. It is a wild area of ancient tamarack bog, forest, grasslands, and lakes. It serves as a generous feeding place for migrating and nesting waterfowl, most notably ring-necked ducks, songbirds, and raptors. Bears dwell in the wooded uplands. Autumn is spectacular here.

Red-winged blackbirds,
Bosque del Apache National
Wildlife Refuge, New Mexico

Autumn reflection

*&yebrow to cattail in marsh weeds
and ever-so-still. I wait in my bag blind on
the sweaty lip of this pool. And then, in the
soot before sunrise, it happens: gadwalls,
American wigeons, wood ducks, and
mallards, so close to me I cannot focus.
Nearby, a raccoon is gently parting the reeds
with the combs of his claws. He bends down
to drink, listens for the message, then looks up
to greet me, face-to-face.*
                                                              J.H.

. . . .

Whitetail deer

In spring and fall, **Montezuma National
Wildlife Refuge** is a veritable traffic jam of
migrating birds. This upstate New York refuge plays
host to thousands and thousands of geese, ducks,
shorebirds, and songbirds, some on their way
elsewhere. Others stay to nest or winter on the
refuge's 6,500 acres of marsh and uplands. Spring
through fall is a great time to visit.

Raccoon

Canada geese in cypress swamp

*O*verhead, geese are pulling winter
from the north, and the sky is a blue-gray
porridge. The wind that riffles the leaves
smells of October, and to my amazement,
the great cypress trees – trunks and all –
are as orange as the leaves on the bottomland hardwoods. There is a place here, in
the center of swamps, that fills with peace-
fulness. A place, where each year, fall is
born again.

K.H.

Cypress Creek National Wildlife Refuge is
part of the southern Illinois Cache River Wetlands
– an extensive cooperative effort to protect and
restore the area's ecosystem. The result is a
distinct blending of remarkable diversity: upland
forests, ancient cypress swamps, bottomland
hardwoods, and the Cache River Wetlands haven
for waterfowl. The massive 1,500-year-old cypress
trees are the oldest living things in the United
States, east of the Rockies.

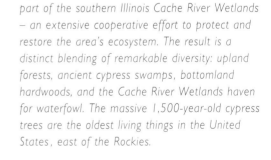

Black-necked stilts

In places like these – where bits of wilderness are surrounded by the stone and steel and jackhammer pace of cities – you can see most clearly the acquiescence of living things. Most of the saltwater marshes have been drained for industrial development, but the wildlife is still here – sandpipers, stilts, and harbor seals, terns, curlews, and California clapper rails. They stand out like sacred icons against the cold, hard edges of daily life. J.H.

California's **San Francisco Bay National Wildlife Refuge** is a conglomeration of tidal salt marshes, mudflats, and sloughs at the southeast end of San Francisco Bay, close to Newark. Black-necked stilts and avocets make their homes here, near the Dumbarton Bridge, year round. Environmental education is a priority on this refuge, where 30 miles of hiking and cycling trails are available to visitors. The entire year is delightful here, but fall is spectacular for shorebird migrations.

Refuge scene

*S*omewhere near Philadelphia, Pennsylvania, sandwiched between the tentacled gridlock of civilization, the hot breath of jumbo jets, and the cold steel of countless commuting automobiles lies this 1,200-acre wetlands oasis at Tinicum. Here, brown-bagging office workers, awed school children on field trips, and even nature photographers stop for just a few moments – to revel in the tranquility of this refuge, sheltered from the frenzy of our world. *J.H.*

John Heinz National Wildlife Refuge at Tinicum, surrounded by bustling I-95 and Philadelphia International Airport, is the quintessential urban "minimart" and reststop for migrating birds. Spring and fall migrations are often extraordinary and include everything from Canada geese and other waterfowl to warblers and shorebirds. The site has been established as a National Environmental Center, where teachers can participate in workshops, and visitors can enjoy the refuge's walking trails.

Rain in the hardwood forest changes everything it touches. Trees gather brilliant greens, and mushrooms and toadstools glisten like new flesh. Syrupy smells of wet wood, old leaves, and tree sap grow so heavy you can nearly fill your pockets with them. Even the light changes with the passage of water, and ordinary stones become glittering garnets and amethysts. Spider webs are strung with pearls. And while the rain falls, I watch silently.

J.H.

Orb spider web

Seney National Wildlife Refuge stretches 95,000-acres in the Great Manistique Swamp of the upper Michigan peninsula. Today, the refuge provides beautiful and richly diverse wildlife habitat – vast, open wetlands for loons, sandhill cranes, northern harriers, and mink. Forests and meadows draw whitetail deer, bear, great horned owls, and sometimes wolves. Plan to visit spring through fall.

Bracket fungi
on sugar maple

46

Fulvous whistling-ducks

all is always bittersweet for me –
the nearness of long winter nights and
Escheresque sunsets, quilted checkerboards
of geese and ducks. A time for reflection and
a rich time for watching waterfowl. Though
this refuge abounds with birds each fall,
fulvous whistling-ducks have been seen only
five or six times in the last hundred years.
Every season has its gifts.

J.H.

. . . .

Blackwater National Wildlife Refuge, *just*
12 miles south of Cambridge, Maryland, is a tidal
marsh haven for migratory waterfowl. The refuge
has become a major wintering area for Canada
geese on the Atlantic flyway, but dozens of other
bird species winter here as well, including mallards,
blue-winged teal, great blue herons, and tundra
swans. Bald eagle sightings are common, and fall is
an excellent time to view these birds.

"Prairie pothole" scene

*A*ldo Leopold knew this place: *"No living man will see again the long-grass prairie where a sea of prairie flowers lapped at the stirrups of the pioneer." The exquisite simplicity of it. Autumn's broad bands of ocher, umber, and tourmaline. And the unrelenting breath of the wind. I want to seize a sense of place, where the ooze of the past becomes the compost under our feet and the prairie arches its back to the stars.* K.H.

. . . .

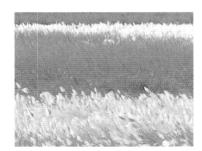

Prairie grasses, Sand Lake NWR, So. Dakota

Named for the Sioux Indian word meaning "nesting place for birds," **Waubay National Wildlife Refuge** is in the major waterfowl migration path of the Central flyway. In the productive prairie pothole region, this northeastern South Dakota refuge has essential upland and wetland habitats for courtship, nesting, and brood-rearing for more than 100 species of birds. The fall colors here are incredible.

Lichen-covered "River of Boulders"

This land is nearly as it was a hundred or more years ago – oak woodlands and mixed grass prairies, bison and longhorn cattle, deer and cougar. Only the shape of the land has changed as water worked and reworked its features, as wind shifted its shape. But the buffalo and grasses are still here, and at night, you can still dance by the light of a thousand-thousand stars.

J.&K.H.

· · · · · · · · · · · · · · · · · · · ·

Texas longhorn

Wichita Mountains Wildlife Refuge in south-west Oklahoma is a large (59,000 acres) and scenic refuge representative of the rugged west. Rolling prairies, steep canyons, gurgling streams, ponds, longhorn cattle, and prairie dogs, this refuge has them all. It also includes a peculiar boulder field – the River of Boulders – dotted with multi-colored lichens. Any time of year, a visit to this refuge is reminiscent of the past.

Winter

*. . . the leaf has grown
no less intricate by its absence.*

*And though it's true that the raven's
black feathers have darkened,*

*the swan's have grown nearly
immaculate.*

❧

*T*he force of life is fiercest in winter. Every movement vital, each choice final. Time itself slows. The northern skies have emptied of birds, and bears have gone to dream the dreams of their ancestors. The stars move closer, and the green skirt of summer falls away. The earth gathers hard and deep brown. And there is wind, like razors. And at the end of it all, the solstice and a place so small you might have missed it, the place where it all begins again.

Unraveling their wings like bolts of Chinese silk, these birds dazzle me this winter dawn. Thousands of mallards have come to this gentle lake to feed and preen. And just when I think they have settled down to rest, some primal wake-up call rockets them skyward, again, smudging the horizon with crimson, teal, gold, and green.

J.H.

· · · · · · · · · · · · · · · · · · ·

Mallards

Wheeler National Wildlife Refuge was created in 1938 from a portion of the Tennessee Valley Authority's Wheeler Reservoir as an experiment. This northern Alabama refuge has become an important and successful wintering locale for tens of thousands of birds, including Canada geese, snow geese, and ducks. Great blue herons and other wading birds also are abundant here in winter, but weather can be severe. Go prepared for cold temperatures.

Snow geese,
DeSoto National Wildlife Refuge,
Iowa

Mallards "exploding"
off the water

Wintering elk herd

Deep winter comes early in Jackson Hole, Wyoming. And the animals quickly settle into their routines. Elk and deer paw at the powdery drifts, golden and bald eagles hunt for mice and hare, and trumpeter swans gather like women in Victorian paintings. But best of all is the sleigh ride across snow-crusted fields, and elk breathing fire into the frozen gray air. J.H.

Bull elk

Established to protect a traditional winter range habitat for elk, the **National Elk Refuge** is primarily in use from November to May. The area provides a welcome gathering spot for about 7,000 elk. Eagles, coyotes, and waterfowl, including a wintering population of trumpeter swans, also use this refuge.

Snowy egret

/nowy egrets have raised the feeding frenzy to an art form. With plumed caps and gold-slippered feet, these stately birds mimic huge wind-up toys at a sunrise pancake breakfast, constantly stabbing the shallow waters for food. The great blue herons have more panache. They quietly pose and wait. At Ding Darling, winter provides a banquet for wading birds – all with their foolish quirks. . . not so unlike us.

K.H.

Red-shouldered hawk

J.N. "Ding" Darling National Wildlife Refuge, founded in 1967, is named for Jay Norwood Darling, a pioneer conservationist and initiator of the migratory bird hunting stamp – the Duck Stamp Program. The refuge's 5,300 acres are located on Sanibel Island, off the southwest coast of Florida. In the winter, the area is known for its egrets, red-shouldered hawks, ibises, wood storks, and roseate spoonbills. But the refuge has a great variety of wildlife year round.

Light-footed clapper rail

𝒯t's a remarkable and pitiful high-wire balancing act I won't forget. At winter's high tide, endangered light-footed clapper rails teetering on bits of floating debris, clinging to branches, and nervously eyeing the feral cats waiting along the sidewalks that rim the refuge. Brick and mortar and the vice of civilization are closing in on the birds' precious coastal salt marsh habitat. J.H.

"Belding's" savannah sparrow

Tijuana Slough National Wildlife Refuge, on the southern tip of San Diego, California's coastline, is home to more than 300 bird species. This small urban refuge – part of the Tijuana River National Estuarine Reserve – was established to protect the threatened and endangered species here, including the Belding's savannah sparrow, least Bell's vireo, and the salt marsh bird's beak plant. An interpretive trail through the marsh provides a good vantage point to view the refuge.

Sunrise at Lacassine Pool

here are armadillos here, fearless and myopic. And there are alligators, old as time itself, raccoons dressed as bandits, whitetail deer, warrens full of rabbits, and skunks fragrant and formidable. But it is the winter birds that bring me here, and the birds that carry me away – at dawn or dusk when the sky fills up with the sun's blood, and flocks of waterfowl move across the light thick as leaves in autumn.

J.H.

Lacassine National Wildlife Refuge *in southwest Louisiana is blessed with a 16,000-acre freshwater pool that draws birds like a magnet. It is a major wintering ground for hundreds of thousands of ducks, geese, and other waterfowl, as well as wading birds, including ibises, roseate spoonbills, herons, and bitterns. Alligators are abundant here. And the swells and whispers of the wildlife symphony are remarkable.*

Sandhill cranes

*W*here sandhill cranes have herringboned their way across the heavens for nearly 40 million years, our refuge love affair began. At Bosque, the dance begins before dawn. Nutmeg brown cranes, mottled snow geese, glossy-backed blackbirds erupting into the air, cranes leaping up from the earth, throwing sticks, uncoiling their necks, and wailing. It's haunting and unforgettable, like the harshness and the beauty of the cycles of life.

K.H.

Sandhill cranes

Established in 1939 to protect greater sandhill cranes from extinction, New Mexico's **Bosque del Apache National Wildlife Refuge** is a magical place, especially in winter. The sandhills have arrived from their Idaho, Montana, and Wyoming nesting grounds to winter in the Rio Grande River Valley. And the refuge's 57,000 acres of marsh, grasslands, and wilderness make this an extra-ordinary place to watch the cranes — sandhills and whoopers — snow geese and wintering raptors.

It's somewhere near 20 degrees below zero, and a stiff wind is working at me from the southwest. My breath gathers in little storm clouds. But even here, where the gnarled hands of weather beat at the land so brutally, there are birds – trumpeter swans, Canada geese, and owls with eyes great enough to see it all. And inside each of our skulls, there is a green vision of summer that we cling to like air itself.

J.H.

Trumpeter swans and Canada geese

Southwest South Dakota's **Lacreek National Wildlife Refuge** comprises close to 16,800 acres of marsh and grasslands. It's an amazing and productive place for waterfowl, including magnificent white trumpeter swans. In summer, the swans and Canada geese nest on the refuge, along with white pelicans, cormorants, and herons. In spring, the area thrums with new bird life, as well as deer, coyotes, muskrats, and beaver.

Short-eared owl

Renewal

*Within each seed lies a cold kernel of death,
within each death the ruby ember of birth.*

❦

*If you look closely – deep within the secret earth, amid winding roots
and hooded worms and pulsing bits of seed – you can see the promise of the
garden to come. The glint of the fluted marigold, the eye of the black-eyed
Susan, the will of the pink Sweet William. And if you listen carefully to the
murmur in the mulch and peer into the pores of rocks, you can receive earth's
amazing gifts: the gaze of the rough-winged swallow, the crown of the cardinal,
and the wing of the dove. All there – waiting.*

Northern rough-winged swallow family,
Protection Island National Wildlife Refuge,
Washington

Refuge Resources

For free information about our nation's refuge system, pick up **National Wildlife Refuges - A Visitor's Guide** *at your local refuge, or write:*

U.S. Fish & Wildlife Service
Publications Unit, MS-130 Webb Building
4401 North Fairfax Drive
Arlington, VA 22203

"Seasons of the Wild" ($23.00)*
or
"Our National Wildlife Refuges"
Calendar ($15.00)*
send check or money order to:

Worm Press
Post Office Box 235
Bellvue, Colorado 80512-0235

or call:
1- 800 / 493-2713
Visa / Mastercard accepted

* Includes $3.05 for shipping & handling